BETWEEN 3D & RHYTHM

THIRTY-FIVE PERSPECTIVES

BY ANNETTE V. CANTU

For my adventurous and loving ones.

Contents

1.) Electronic Spatial Integrity by Annette V. Cantu	3
2.) Forensic Science 8.0 Version by Annette V. Cantu	5
3.) 8 Driftwoods by Annette V. Cantu	7
4.) Angel Soundbites by Annette V. Cantu	9
5.) Romancing the Duels by Annette V. Cantu	11
6.) Ribbon of the Forests by Annette V. Cantu	13
7.) Dignity of the Lance by Annette V. Cantu	15
8.) Surround Sound Justice by Annette V. Cantu	17
9.) Might Be My Last by Annette V. Cantu	19
10.) At the Crisp of Daybreak by Annette V. Cantu	21
11.) Who would have thought? By Annette V. Cantu	23
12.) Verge of Drought by Annette V. Cantu	25
13.) Spectacle of Prisms by Annette V. Cantu	27
14.) Tenth Time not the Charm by Annette V. Cantu	29
15.) Rebounding from Top by Annette V. Cantu	31
16.) Unnecessary Sacrifice by Annette V. Cantu	33
17.) Wish I could sue you by Annette V. Cantu	35
18.) Hardbound Meet by Annette V. Cantu	37
19.) Erupted Vortex by Annette V. Cantu	39
20.) Under the Oxygen in Water by Annette V. Cantu	41
21.) Forever with Valuable Conditions by Annette V. Cantu	43
22.) Delectable Firestorm Delight by Annette V. Cantu	45
23.) Children of Valencia City by Annette V. Cantu	47
24.) Ninth Worldly View by Annette V. Cantu	49
25.) From Prayer to You by Annette V. Cantu	51
26.) Love Echoing Us by Annette V. Cantu	53
27.) Didn't Expect their Kind by Annette V. Cantu	55
28.) A Finer Life than Mine by Annette V. Cantu	57
29.) Searching Beyond My Skin by Annette V. Cantu	59
30.) Central Law's Touch by Annette V. Cantu	61

Electronic Spatial Integrity

That blue moon beams with the light of a thousand reflections per second
While we wait for the earth to make its course above the celestial thought.
It's impossible to forget the duties the human race beckons.
As the green blades raise to the sun kissed sky and as the grape vines on limbs stalk.

The days aren't numbered while my neighbor drinks from the endless water
When I lay my seed down, more gyres of decoction arise from mother's womb
The breath of the heart knows the hard day's work that will not falter
For what is fostered is for my neighbor above or below any deep tomb.

Just before the lid closes for the tiresome eye
A song builds and contracts with the night crystals
A sound that can't be ignored and raises the ear to the stars in the sky
The cool breeze lifts the spirit to find another hidden connection before it falls.

Rest assured my feet plant solidly on abundant stable ground
The dreams come to fruition as each blend another successful monumental idea
My spirit keeps churning while life moves on
The dignity to have, and perseverance to know I will overcome any path entwining each realm.

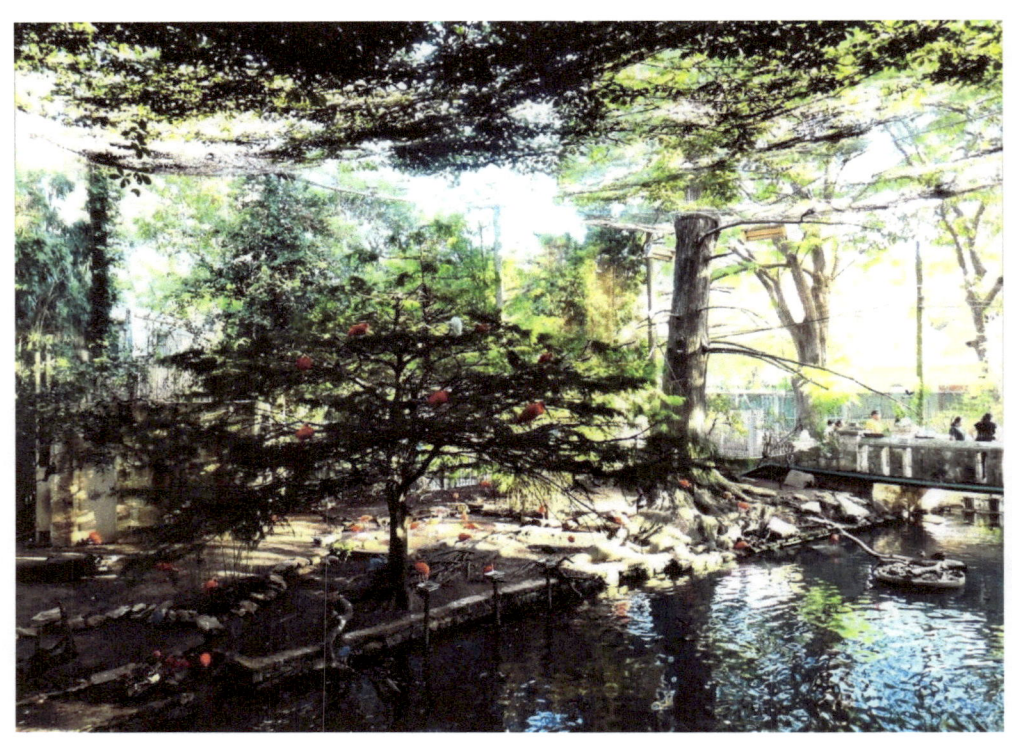

Forensic Science 8.0 Version

The details may get away for now.
Yet, my friend that speaks high above the earth who breathes the dreadful smell
And eats the tiny abundant scavengers that investigate the fresh scene around another town
Will always pass on the true message to the next living soul who is ready to listen well

After each cataloged age-document, and before each new scientific fact
Lays the urgency to put the truthful pieces together for the lady with the balancing scales
The work continues on the machines of the functioning respiratory system on track
When one story is complete, another starts on the heels of the latest without fail.

Our history builds with each new future's twist of fate
That doesn't deter the natural good in us all
Despite the decay of the timeless colosseum's irreplaceable space
Safely moving forward with the entire current civilization among glass walls.

Ideas may be approached with diversity
And the sky may sometimes be the limit.
However, everyone's voice wants to ring the tune freely.
As long as the pathways are clear to resolve each story and as each part fits.

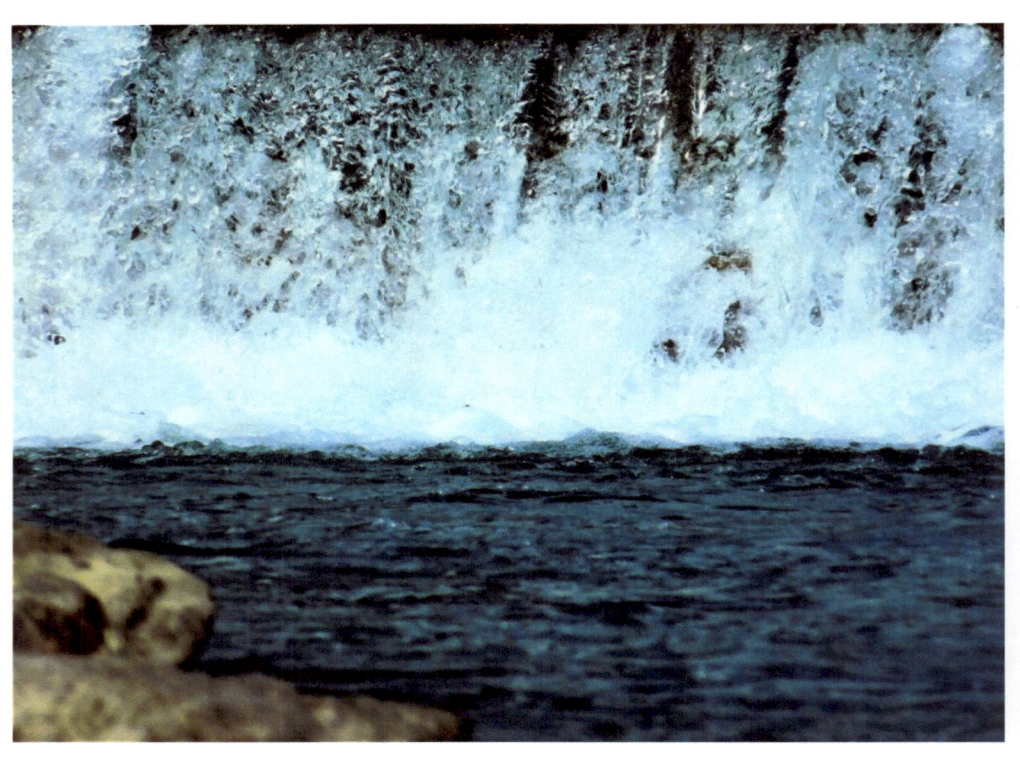

8 Driftwoods

Feeling the beat from left to right while taking in the sweet song for thought
Smooth, colorful, and transitional elements sweep the hands
Tiredness brings the fading scene onto the viewed world tautly
This place is unforgettable and throughout life this place is branded

Near the surface and Far from sight
Emotions are moving north, east, south, and west
Magnetic poles balance the tranquility inside
Without the equilibrium the soul would be useless

Hear the silence of waves
Fine tune the humming from each magnetic pulse to oneself
The rock swings with ease when weightless
Let the tumultuous mix of feelings release by the surface's tilt

Another red star, and a blue star around Orion's traditional belt
Another soaring youthful creature far from sight
Letting the deep, dark, lands pull my gravity to destiny and tell
How good it is to feel the blessings of life's delight.

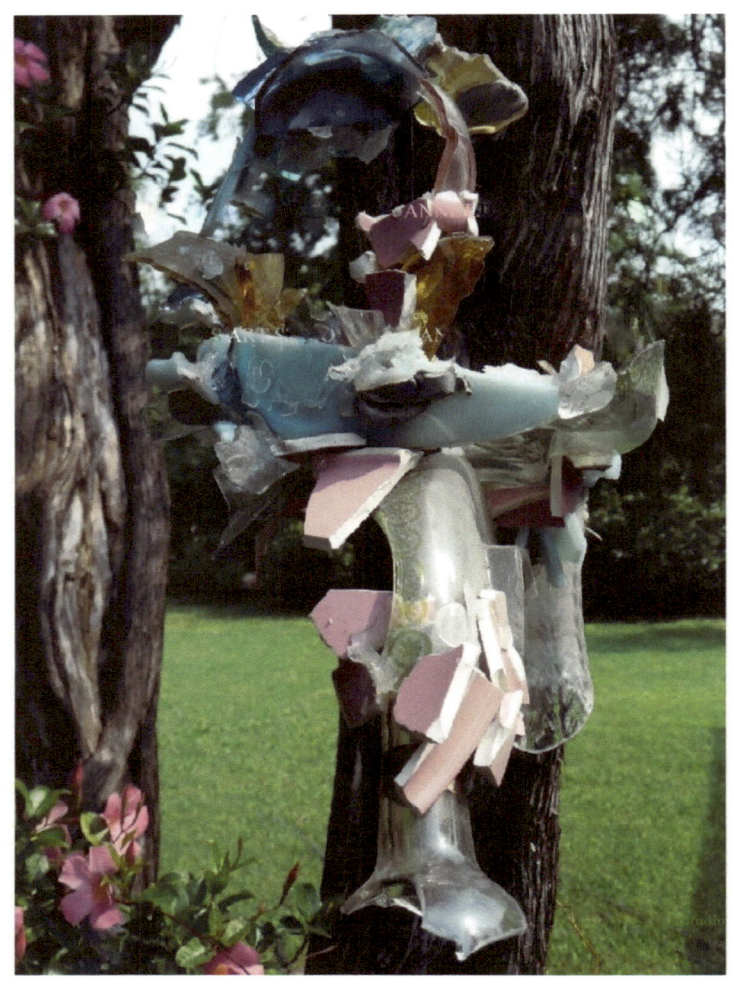

Angel Soundbites

Midnight words ring with sweet joy
Spurring feelings from thoughts of children playing to basking during brunch
About to burst from so much laughter and nestle with the conversations coined
Air of wonder inspires a forlorn and forgotten sense of awe's touch

Even when the atheist doesn't know the reprieve from prayer
A heart is beating for the movement of another
Kindness continues to thrive by the multiplied population and weaves each other
Into another gracious presence of the valuable dreamer.

While the forces of the galaxy changes and the air supports the desert rose
The soft whispers comes gently on the freshly shivers of cool void less space
Guidance cloaks the surface to point in the successful direction among humble abodes
Never a second goes by unnoticed with love and grace

When it might just be too dark to settle for a slow step
The nightly firefly pokes to find a quick rejuvenating drink and gives a hint of light
Our shoulders, under a full day's sigh, rest
Under salvation's wings and a mindful eye

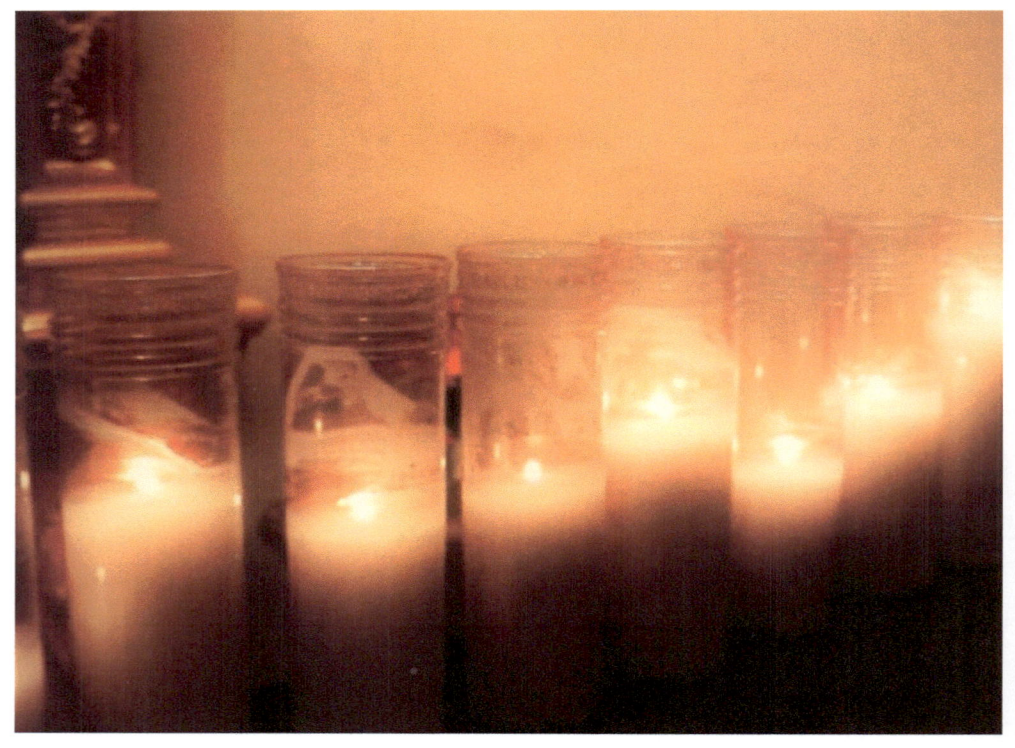

Romancing the Duels

He faltered, she cried under the vibrations of the Nano second sonic booms
A historical tale of a fateful morning when the weeping willow trees towered
Messages meant for only the lover's ears with encaptivating tunes.
Will never forget the Black Queen's meeting with the White King.

The gentleman of the west met the gentleman of the east, July fourth
While the families met in the middle from north and south to witness their sleep around the event
Markings on the ritual grounds hinted very well of the future's course
When the moment became tinged with another's corruptive sense

The two were not supposed to meet, and when the unexpected flight took place
Backs faced an unforgiving journey
After the rooster's first croak and the people became awake
Every activity sprung to life on unpaved, and uneven streets.

As the steps drew nearer to make one last step
The turnabout met with a crackling sound on slightly lit skin.
As the truth seared on the red as the liquid poured out on green beds.
Love poured over the souls before the meet with hopes, before the dark dimmed.

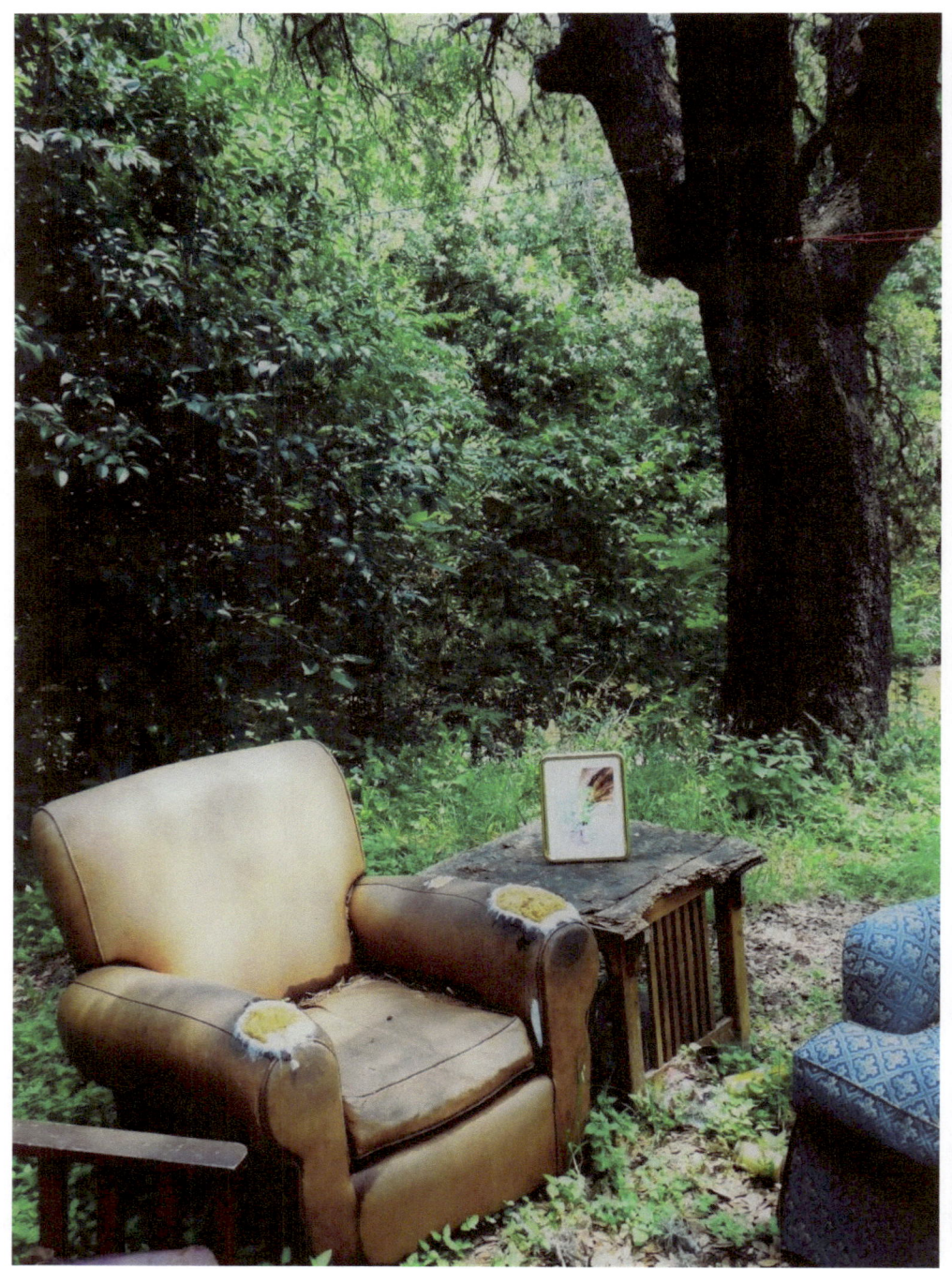

Ribbon of the Forests

A child spoke the words of a story
Starting with the beautiful maiden of the forest
Whom shouldn't be ignored, due to her light's glory
There was an eventful day, when his bird laid to rest.

She heard the melody, and brought tears to beak
The pain was so loud, she felt weak, and barely breathed
The shallow wind was steady, and with slow heartbeats
His bird laid in hand and lungs heaved.

Master spoke of the raging lands
No one risked their lives when the earth cracked
His message for his enemies to listen, to not be damned
As she began to realize, majestic tides could not pull back

Quickly, overcoming the blooming nature
The fading ribbons of smoke from embers
There, the baby laid, from what was left from old timbers
His bird brought a family together

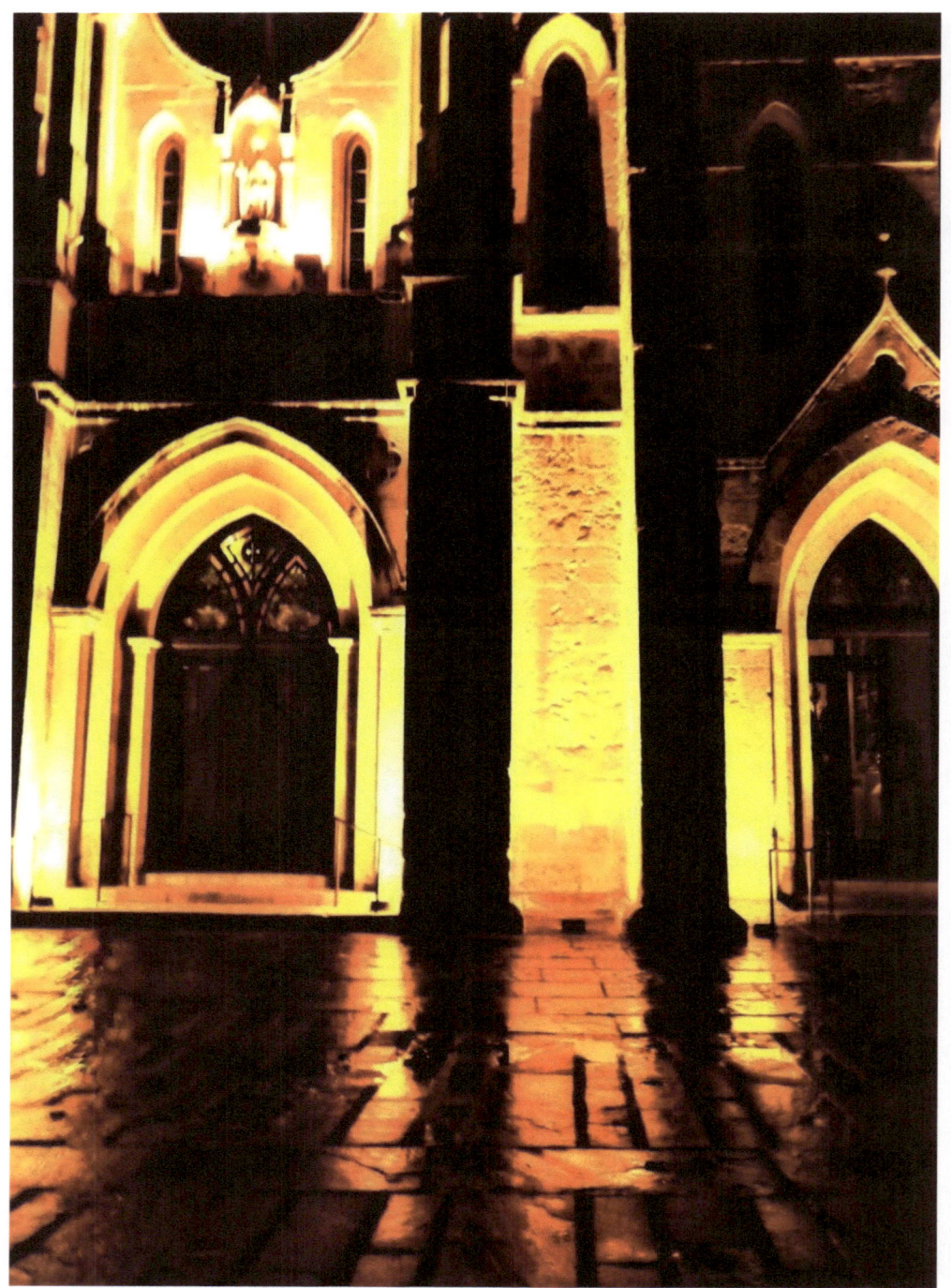

Dignity of the Lance

Under the hot molten pour of stainless steel.
The aged crucible holds the cup of liquid so well.
Sulfurous steam rises as the form takes shape when it keels
Sizzling sounds and sputters of gaseous bubbles bursting from the swell

Seconds, hours, and days of synchronized sanding to refine the surface
The sister's cool reflection show's a peaceful family resemblance
One layer at a time is adjusted to prepare for the world's changing visual image
Finding the suitable hands for a historical bearer's weight.

Understanding foresight's shadow
Balancing the sides of justice with others
To not let fear cripple and be deterred by the dark thoughts of someone.
Sleeping awake and walking with Dicaeosyne's powers.

Accept the moment to yield the protective strike
Dismiss the doubtful inquiries over freedom's bridge
Let evil and anger intersect on its own platform to die
Seizing the hard reality to give rise and lift

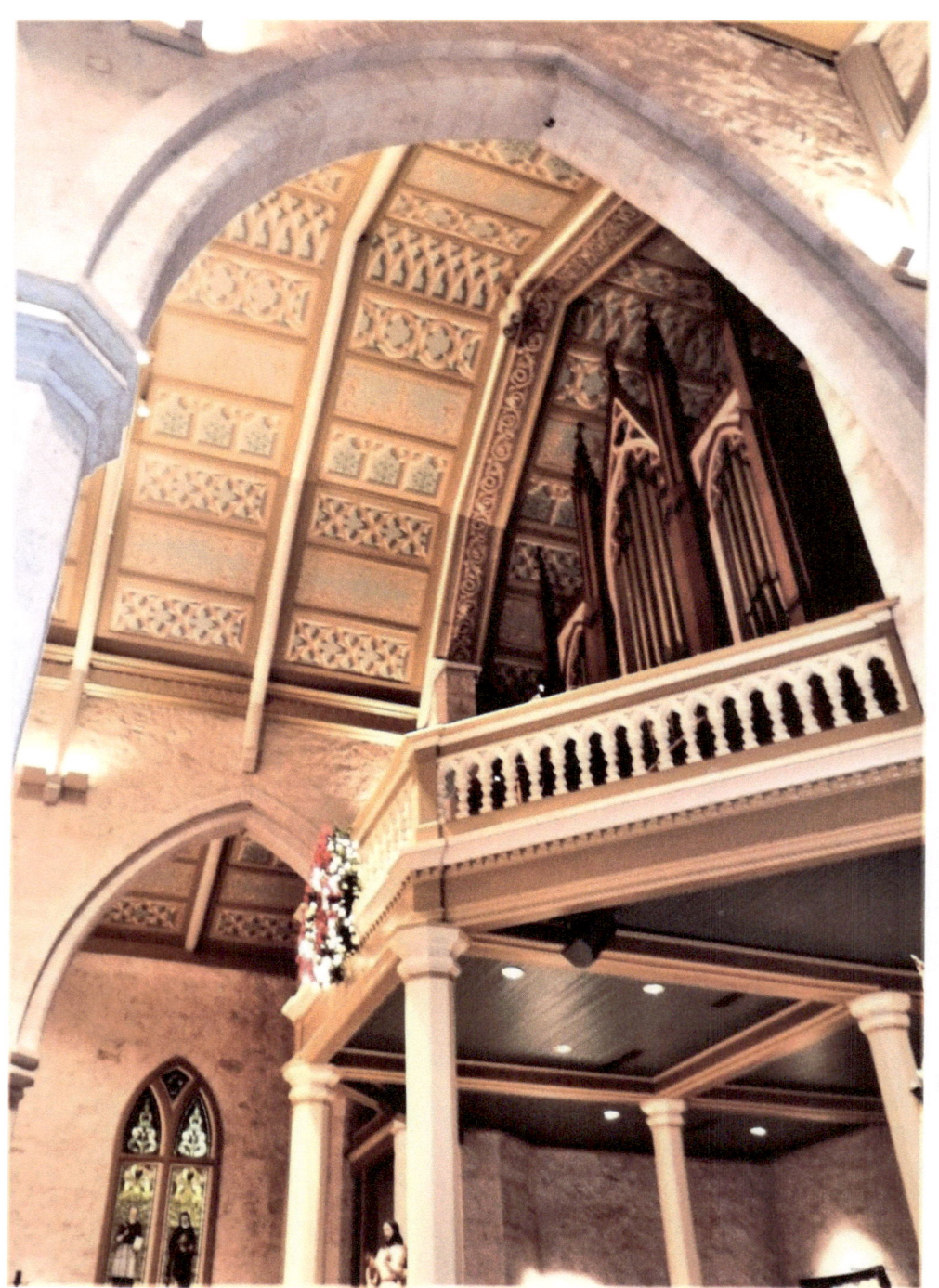

Surround Sound Justice

A room with no walls on grounds full of color.

The rain pours on trees to trickle water onto the man's fountain.

Winds blow the echo of chatter and baked goods swirl around the senses together

Don't let the cricket that plays its tune fool you at the bottom.

Court's ruled the political outcomings

Voices, silently, stated the daily opinion

Occasionally watching the tea and coffee pouring

Leaves move out of the corners and rodents' ashes.

Heat rises from available chimney stacks

The garden is treated with nutrients and water

Cluster of gnats

Monarch season is nearer

Musicians play on the jazziest porch

Artists display their heartfelt images

Technology increases the humming of signals for daily reports

Silence is my uniquely rare distant friend

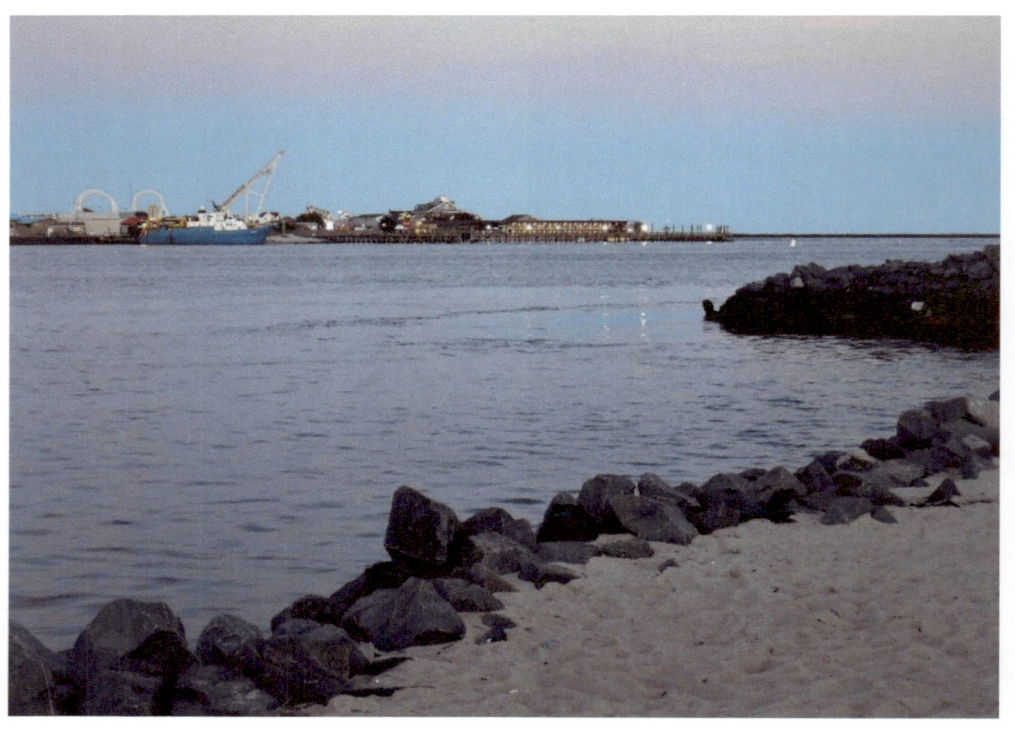

Might Be My Last

The look in his strange eyes that told a million histories

Sipping the red vintage and for a moment went back in time

Crisp air blushes the cheeks and I breathe

Ecstatic from the glistening lights that dance from the strums of keys.

Beautiful people unaware of the happiness beaming from inside

Sharing the feelings of warmth to foreign ears.

Night falls only on the cold fingers of a goodbye

By the simple lantern an old, soft, scarf of dried tears.

A message flickers across the mind while gazing on love.

A couple speaks under spiritual wings.

Life is valuable and our fates are not locked.

Building a dream on what our words speak.

Gorgeous tints radiate of a natural gift.

Markings of grace.

Should I sit?

My place.

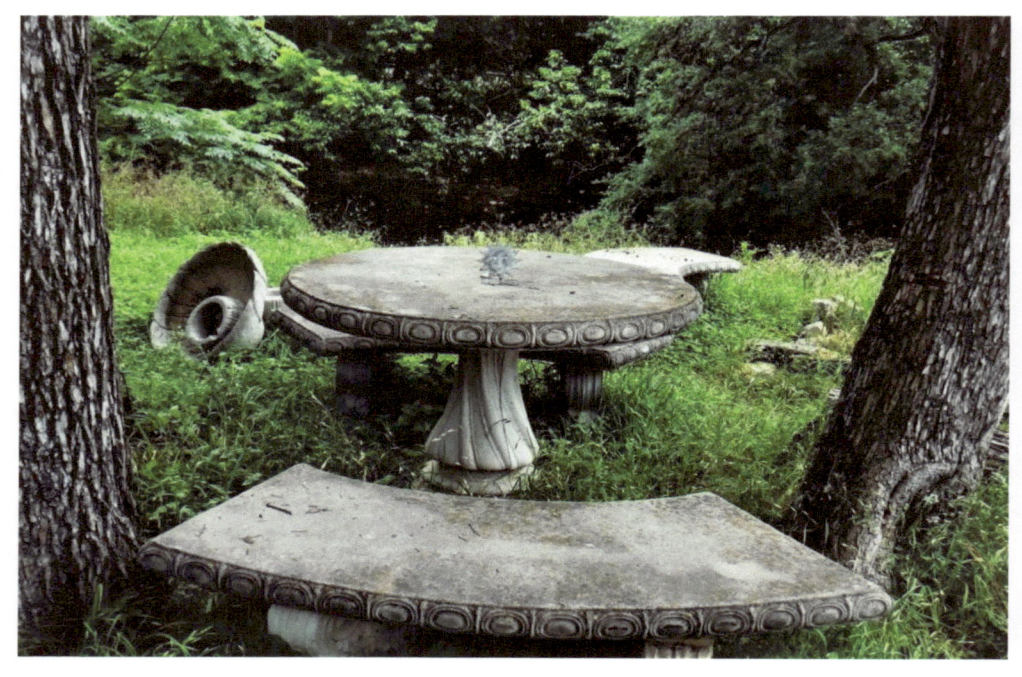

At the Crisp of Daybreak

My body stretches and yearns for the sun's warmth.

Getting ready for the sprints and marathons.

Clouds part the way, no storms, and will go forth.

Chasing the night dreams, where we long.

Departed Souls greet the love growing earth's seeds

Forgiving the steps that trampled unknowingly on grounds under stars.

Witnessing the beauty between light and dark seams

Honoring those, allowing me to see freedom on wooden beams that are carved.

Letting the past be the past while the historical monuments still stand

Letting the day rotate over my spirit toward successful progress

Baring down the unruly pressures the thieves that band

Undeterred to a new day with a few new stresses.

Unsettling the dark whispers to move on in the light

Binding the earth to prosper under steady streams

Careful acts when tending to other's business in mind

Before the day is over, for my brother and sister, I breathe a sigh of relief.

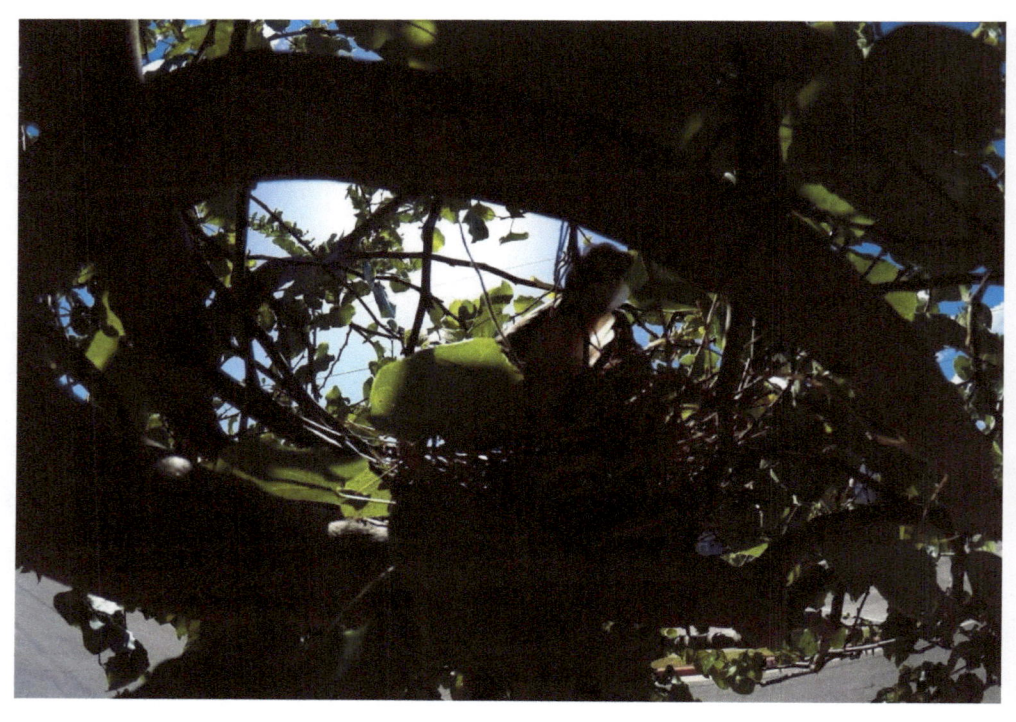

Who would have thought?

The day would be filled with tears of pain and joy
My children play, dance, and sing on freedom's ring
The water is fresh, welcoming, and on a hot day cold
Then, my love is caged among the devilish soul's darkest ravines

Several thousands of gifts filled the old cottage
The winter storm brought snowflakes and warm white chocolate
Leaves changed color before we knew it
Then, as I sat at a public table and a stranger sat in front of me.

All the roses and specialty flowers give the sweetest scent
Kitten's kisses, puppy's kisses, and butterfly kisses send love
Delicious meals cooked well by professional chefs
A random message falls on my lap from above

Dear Love, I haven't forgotten about you while away
To see your happiness grow and success bloom
Knowing your spirit is not forgotten and you are doing ok
Didn't realize how much love there was for me, from you

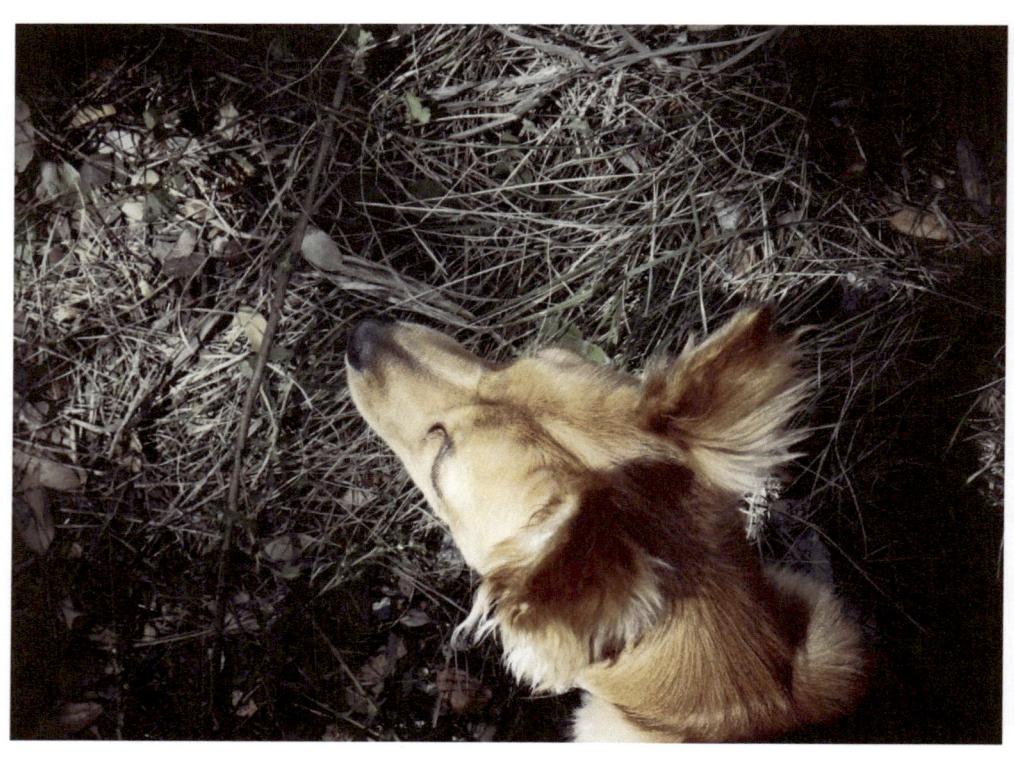

Verge of Drought

Parched lands on babbling tongues of neighbors
When the birds fly high above the terrain far from the bays
Sands mound high, building dunes between territories
He will stand next to her, He is miles apart each day

Even as the drought starts to set
We know our story we tell to each other
On land lines deteriorating and with frays
Surrounded by books becoming fragile, books to pass onto our sisters and brothers.

My flowers will not wither, due to the freeze
Your trees will not fall, due to the stormy rains
He that cuts down trees, can't see the lack of seeds
She that hinders water to the flowers, can't see the lack of humid air and warm rays

The words linger dryly before the speaker
Ears gather to listen for the profound ending
Alone starts to be the friend when desperately reaching for another
Finally, it arrives, the savory feeling before the drink.

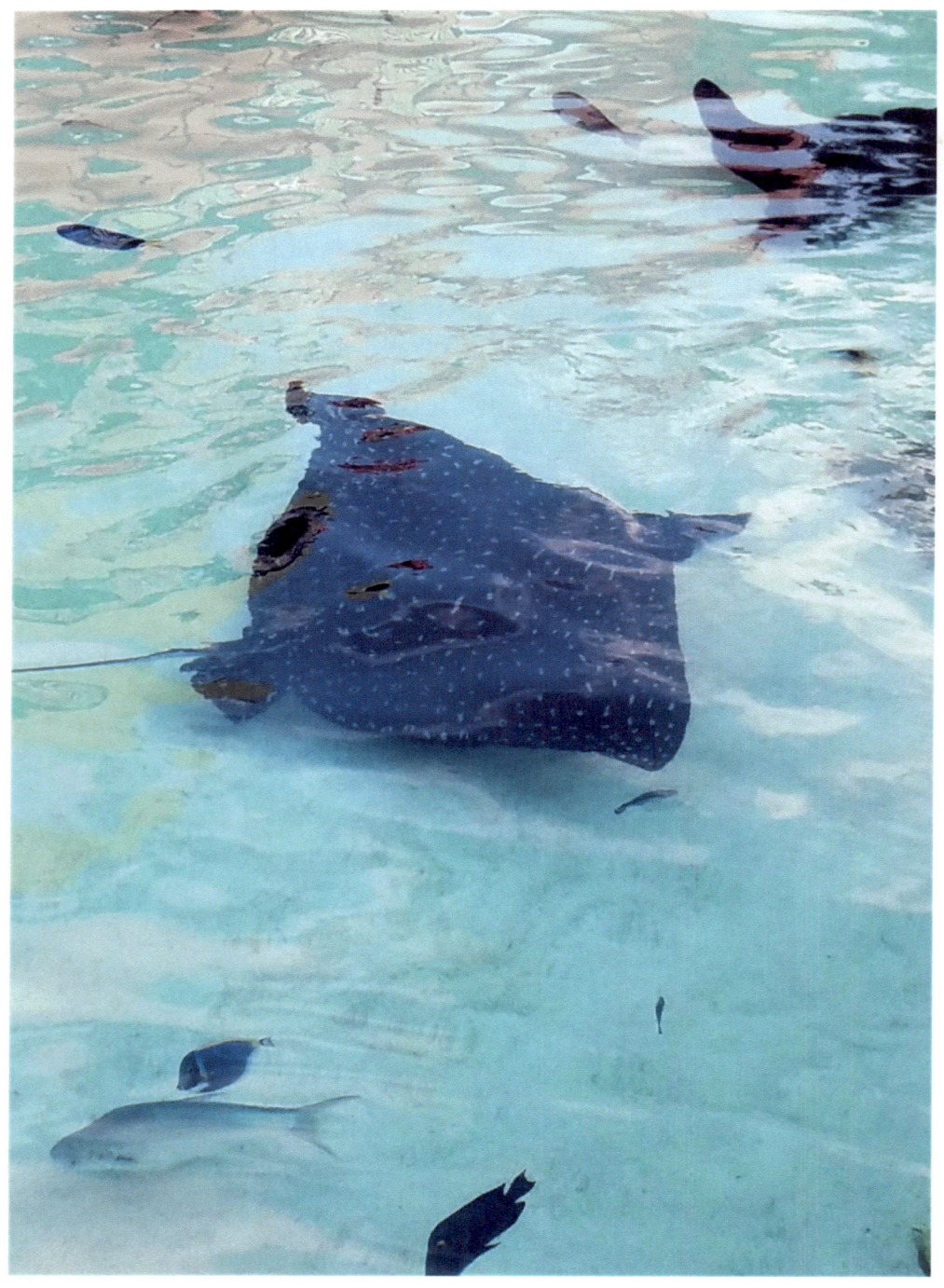

Spectacle of Prisms

He smiled and sincerely greeted me with kind words.

She made a joke that made me fill with warm laughter.

Little child poked at the new object until curiosity was null and void.

Little child stated clearly how the sky moves as we walked freely together.

Even the darkness shed its neon and varied glows.

Animals howled to a different tune before the sunrise.

Cold and spacious lands colored the landscapes to speak the untold

Daring animation continues to thrive and work the black night

Various interests surface on unknown platforms

When the time passes on, nobody is able to clearly connect with technology

Human variety is valued and cherished enough for the performance

What matters the most is being apart each musicality

Welcoming the blessed whispers

Living among the spirited beings

Sleeping on the trusting hands as each galaxy stirs

Wearing the multicolored screens, while sipping on ginger tea.

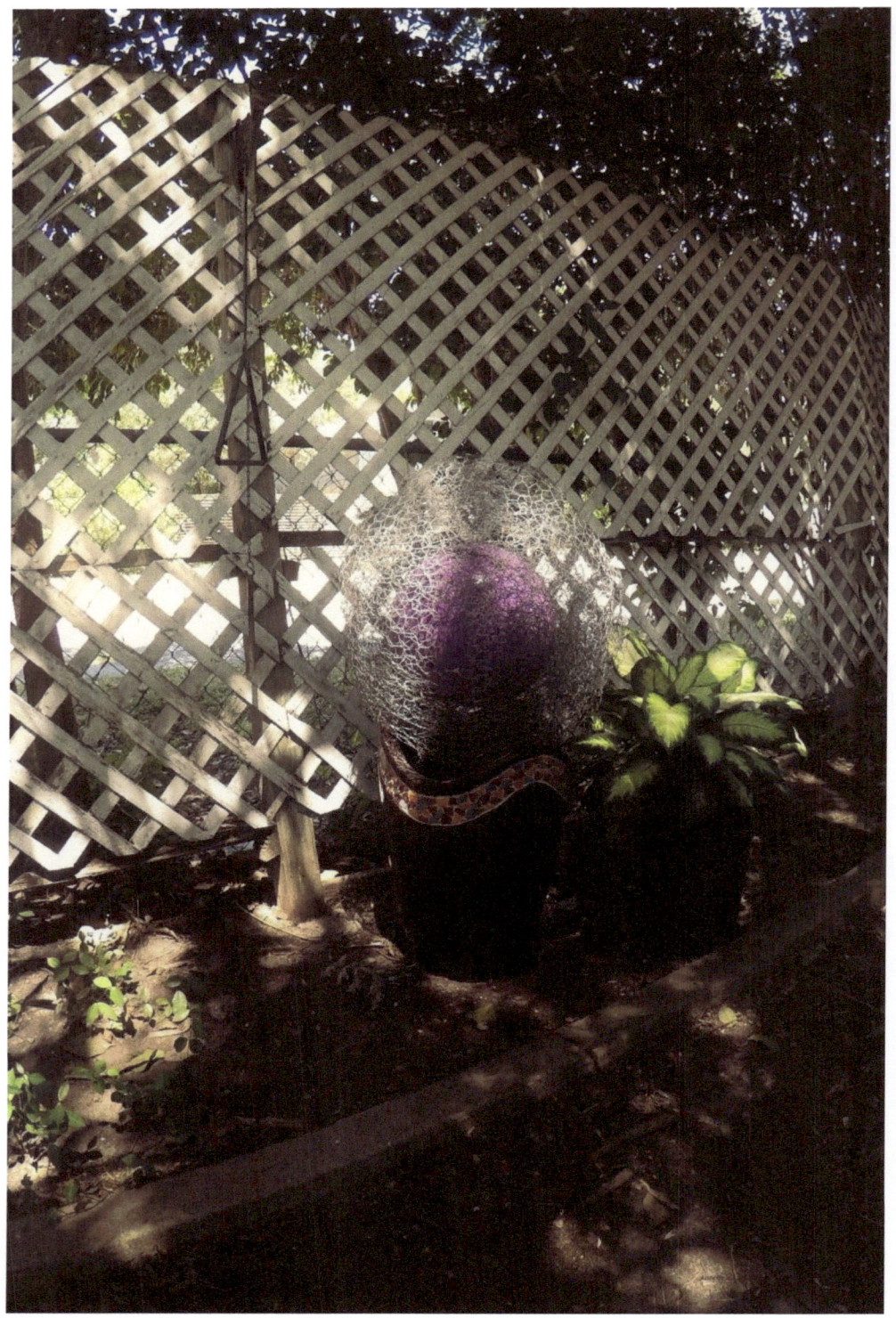

Tenth Time not the Charm

Every time, the coffee would not mix to the right concentration
Instructions paralleled abstracts and given fractions of every object
The person that met me today, was another friend for a different reason
Could have stayed with my love if he had let me and help me mend.

First time was supposed to be fine, after following respectable rules
So tried again, again, with truthful sounds, again, again, and again.
Reflected on prehistoric wisdom conversational tools
Took into consideration the futuristic sayings

After forgiving, again, it seemed as if my freedom was being prevented so that I may be me.
Knowing my sense in life without breaking any laws
Again, tried to find the relational umbilical cord to another human being.
It's there with the almighty above, with the healing spirit provides free will of all.

So listening to the married maidens and remembering traditional values.
Taking into consideration the successful veterans of war, the survivors.
Again I tried after another cleansing of rituals
Again, realizing the love in me and for me as a gift to go on through the heaven's door.

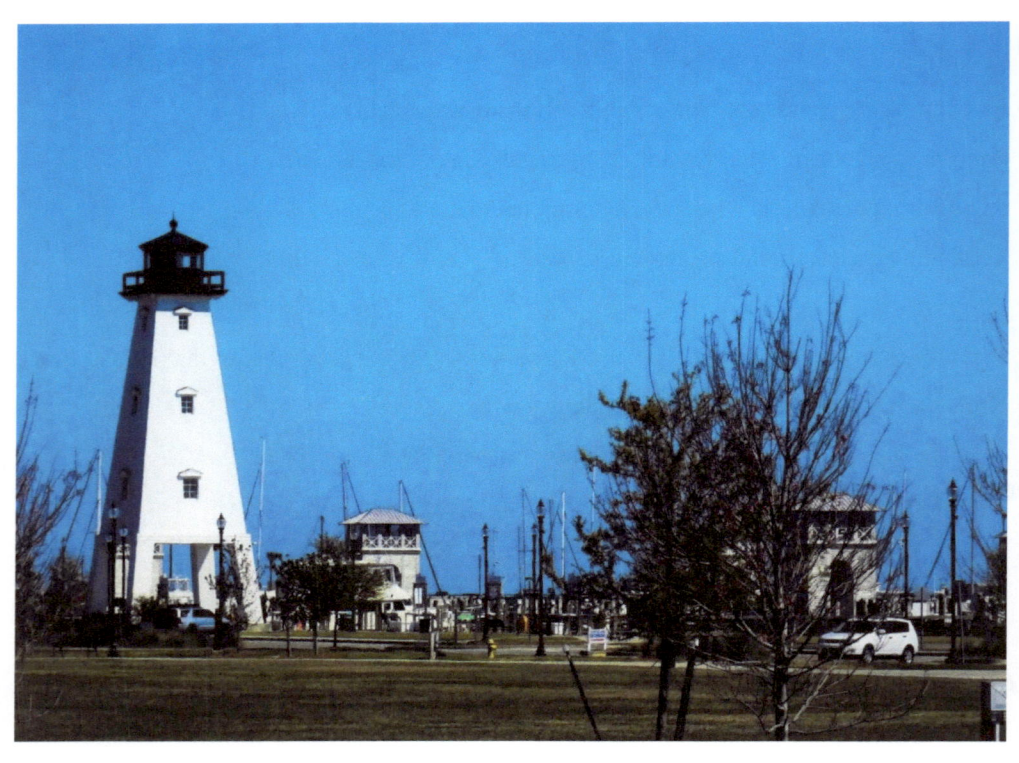

Rebounding from Top

It is refreshing to see, hear, taste, touch, and smell the clear air.

Bouncing between realms of each unique person's viewpoint.

Gaining momentum in knowledge with understanding, when one does dare

To take on the challenge of adventure for anyone to join.

Never falling from above an Angel's view from holy art

Always jumping over the tiny devil like bumps

Feel free to always connect while we each play are favorite parts

Try not to slam into the concrete slab, and avoid the dreams to be crushed.

Alive is the key for the spirit and the heart

Flight and weightless provides the much needed safety net

Continue to bend to the fluctuation of nature's metamorphose structure.

The space to reside in houses the nurturing for help to not transgress.

From one untouched step to another

Fostering a new self and rejuvenating

Staying at peace to understand arising, exterior, conflict from a misunderstood world.

Resolve continues to help me reach the top frequently.

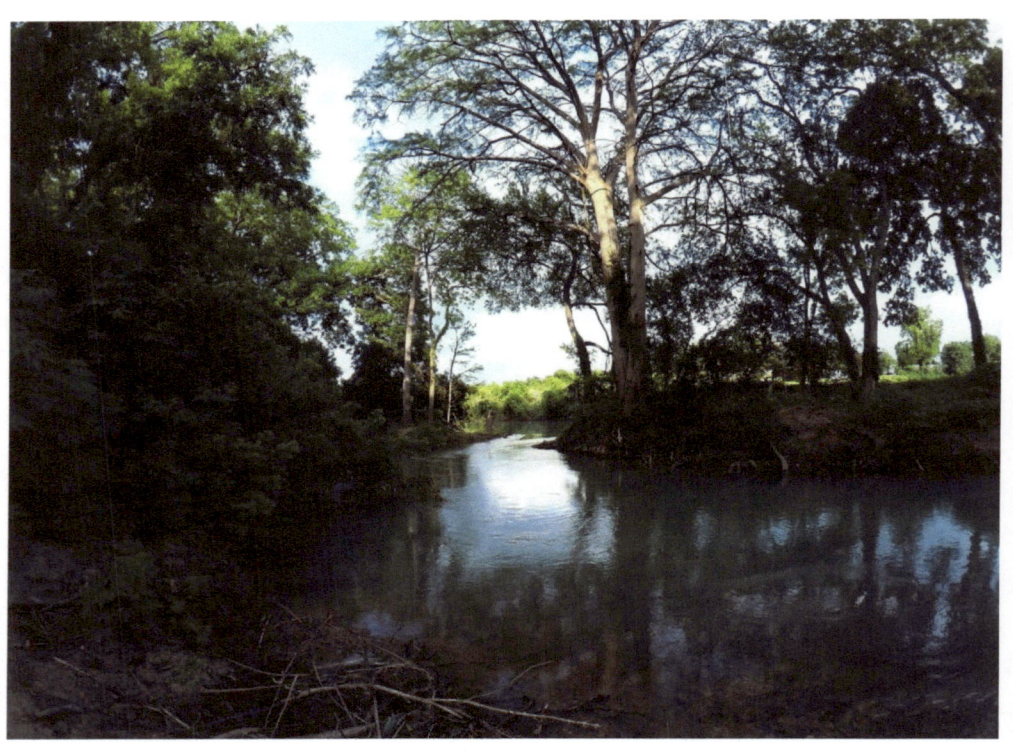

Unnecessary Sacrifice

It's strange when the liars keep lying even when being viewed through tests
The same misunderstanding effects any quality of life
When the book pages turn so does the silence from the passing good reflects
Another perspective to shed mandatory light

The fluttering of the baby bug's wings hold still a sight
Fawns gallop and stride by the head of the lineage in the pack
Working with the sea's tides
Hands reflect the soul's mission and strength in a good courageous stance

A majestic trait written on our skins that is risky to tamper with
Scars tell a story of different kinds and hold different meanings
Unborn necessities hold more fruit for her and him
Unheard and heard messages matter for unique reasons

Balance of deeds for the self and others
Important life circumstances keep us all going
The life in the eyes helps make the connection easier
Don't waste another cause, unjustly.

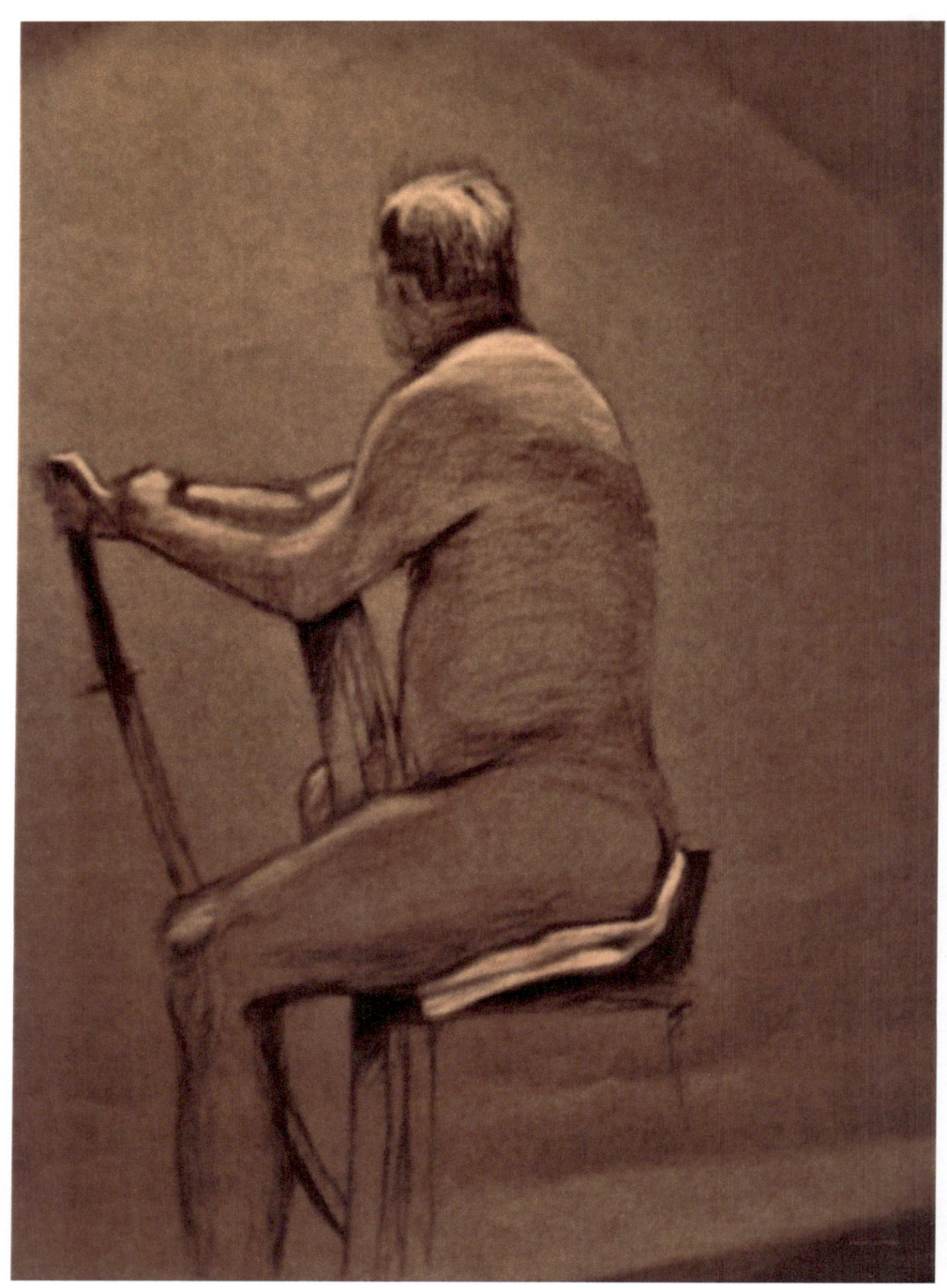

Wish I could sue you

Often has the saying been mentioned "Patience is a virtue"[1]
My ears, eyes, and my attention are always for you
Yet, the days when scorching verbiage pours from another stranger
To the point my good soul from the Lord starts to ponder what is spewed

The foul language drenches the air, soils the media, and damages all blood.
Greed attaches to the rumors and fills the gluts of the automatic copycats.
Continuous negative attitudes serve the self-conceited and the pompous alone.
Judgmental engagement only becomes detrimental on those who cause the latest gag.

Children will waste valuable time if the focus is to not support their land.
Unseen damages will only return in the future to be dealt with again.
The feeling is amazing when support really does happen.
Focusing to honor our ancestors will help future country growth to stand.

So, why all the bickering and distasteful regards to simple issues?
Every puzzle is meant for personal growth not forced conquering.
The individual wars can end and each goal will rise anew.
My life is just as valuable as yours and we both must endure the clashing rings.

1. Proverbial phrase written in 5th century

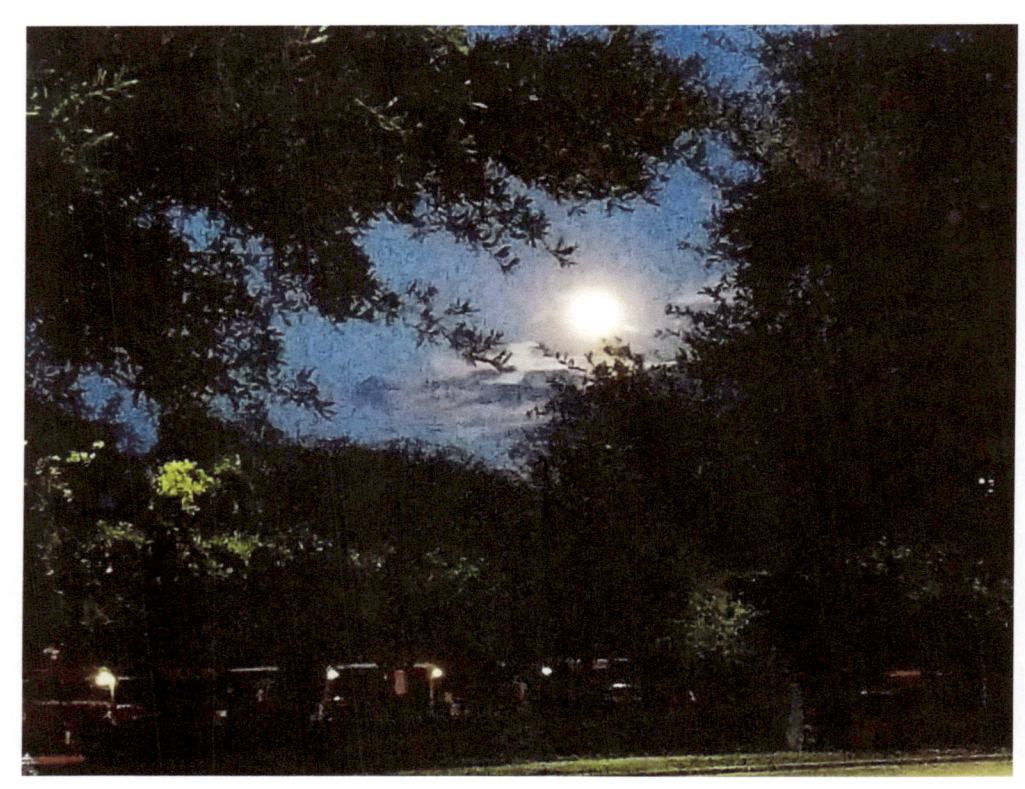

Hardbound Meet

Beautiful is your look, and your presence is greatly appreciated.

When you join me alone or in public.

The security of your knowledge.

Provides the comfort I enjoy for every informational non-sequential clip.

My interests are always perked.

You lead me to new depths and soaring heights.

Forgiveness is your key success and closure resolves the old alerts.

Binding all time to any given moment on hand with delight.

It is for you my memory serves me well.

The help of many from the past to find success in the future.

An understanding that we share, as the truth always tells.

Paths through all provisions help me strive and live better.

Always grateful as the words unfold from the innocent off the pages past

Staying in sync with your tune

Adjusting to newfound perspectives and challenges that will last

Knowing I will be best with you.

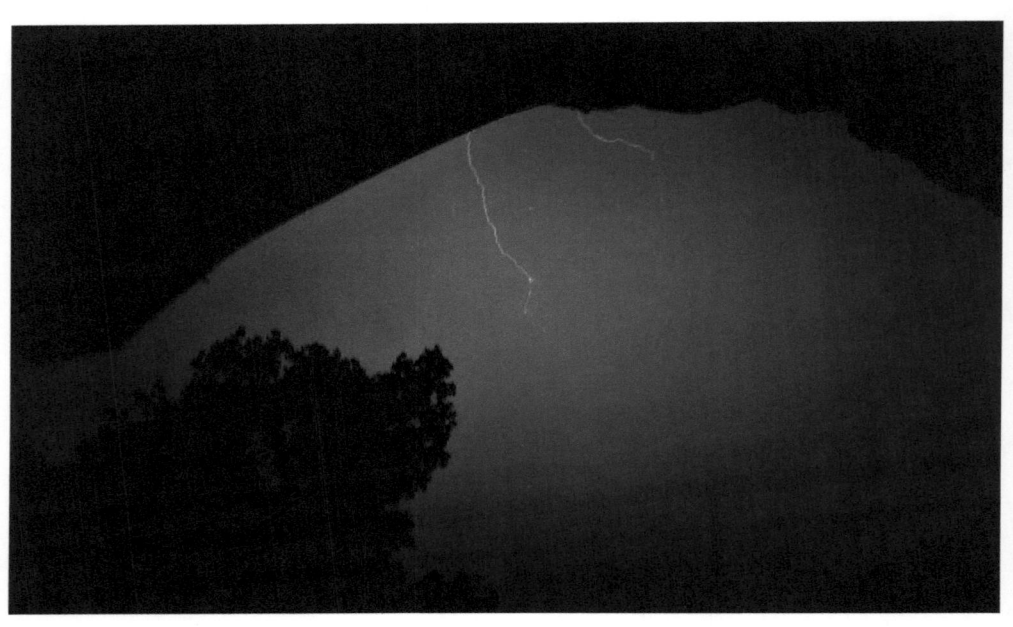

Erupted Vortex

All this time I thought the world was safe

Then the pain flowed for no reason

My happiness filled the organic lifeforms inhabiting the place

After the fact, would have thought there would be better situations

Yet, words from the holy dreams arrived

My colorful pictures explained those few corruptions

Love nestled in me to arise

Rare people who are tainted with darkness behind light blue eyes disrupt

My palette provides warmth, goodness, and forgiveness

If it weren't for the blood borne heroes of past in the veins

The lights would have faded

My bed is always on the backs of angel's wings

While I pick up the broken pieces of the world

Respect has found me on the edges of shards

Air warms and cools after the morning's gesture

Don't come to me with hurtful sounds from distant Lords of dark.

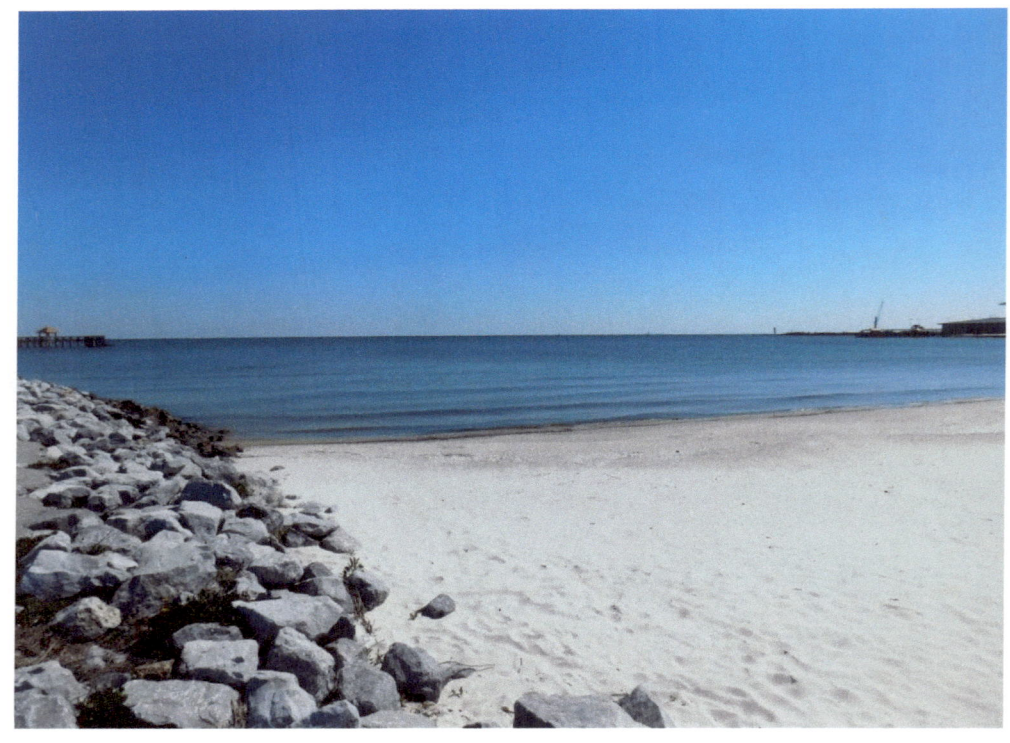

Under the Oxygen in Water

Haven awaits with the awe

Between two outstretched mountains topped with flying whooping cranes

On the soils of stagnant, old, battlefields fall

The secure bridge cascades down to connect the future and past tense

The way was shown with vivid colors of all the fish in the seven seas

Rejuvenated by the coral filled waters

While floating under the waves of light filtered through the trees

To finally see the truth past the foggy blue, so stark

Before my eyes could lift to the bobbing clouds

A horn on a boat on a distant path steadily plunged forward

The joy from the people's entertainment channeled through loud

When the party reached the calm shores to bring another on board.

In a panic, the leaves draped around by the surprise

The air felt soft and the flowers bloomed their scent

The huge structure presenting itself to me as it slowed the stride

Movement stirs in nature's beauty and I cried less.

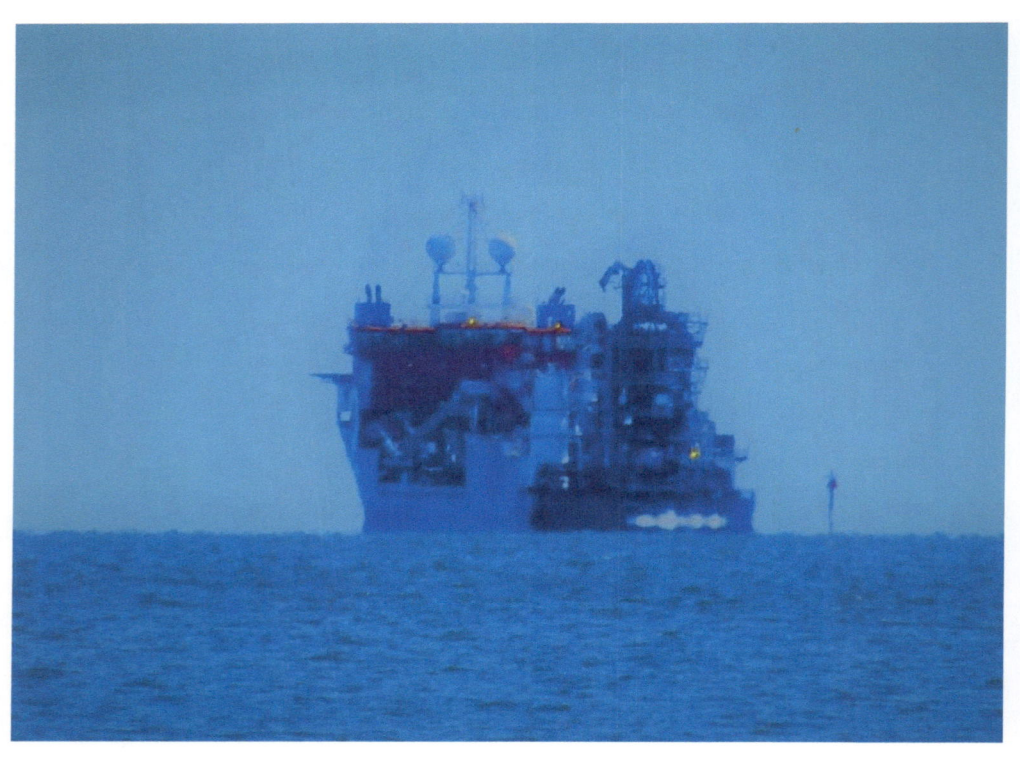

Forever with Valuable Conditions

Unsurmountable quantum energy kinetically entwined with the gulp of fresh juice
Just as he has promised, an infinitive fulfillment.
Allowing each sole to freely roam to reap the fruits
With days of understanding to pay the price with forgiveness

One mark will always transform on another
While walking the trails of universal time
How treasurable the growth of the carvings bind together
The growth of the brilliant white strand of hair cascades from life's tide

She followed through on spiritual's grace
Knowing the gift will be well-deserved
The heritage plays music for each newborn to hear at each pace,
To play the commitment for those who be willing to understand the leverage

Even in dreaming the food is garnished with the same type of flower
Forever holding the true colors that isn't falsified
Always bearing the love where physical eyes are unable to see there
Creating from the platforms of a sacred birthright.

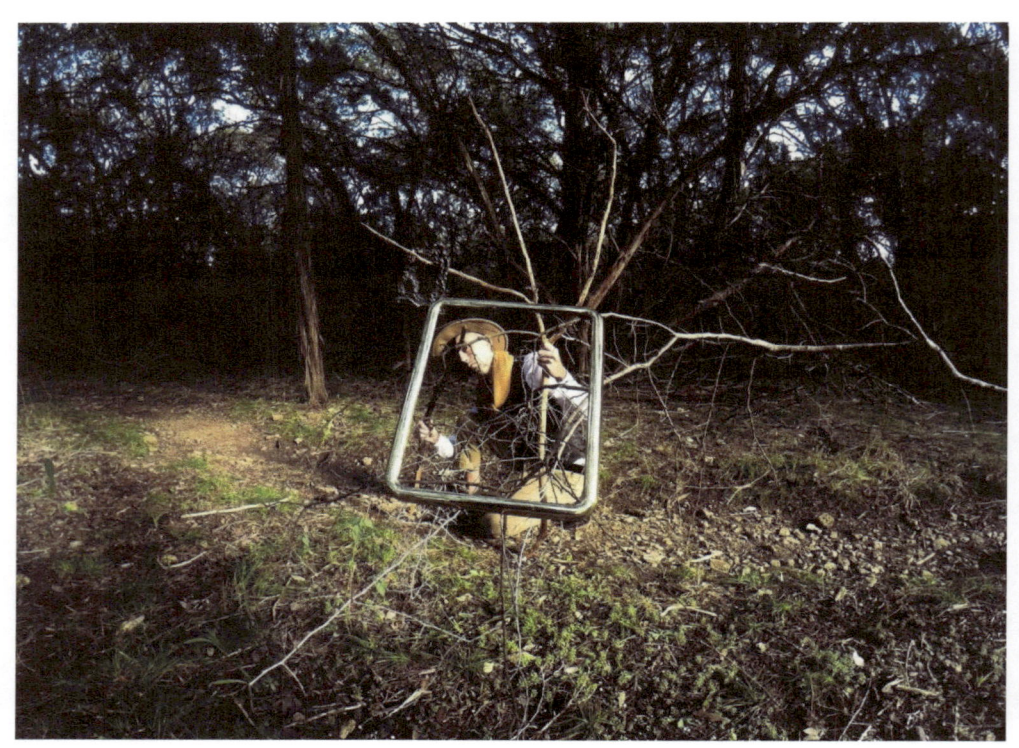

Delectable Firestorm of Delight

Drinking enchanted water alongside bottlenose dolphins

Love brought on by a stranger's sincerest

Lucid, aquatic, lights tinge the soul's giggles

Electric cords fog below footsteps discreetly

The meal that was served to me had labels of honor

Words spoken with reverence from endearing friends

Some dimes add for another year's warmth in winter storms

Head rests on marshmallow layers helping breathe in energy

Sounds of beauty's gift blankets my safety

Mountainous shadows cool the hot winds on eyelids

Seers bless my ears for lover's pleasure and tears

Day explodes with stars' waves and celestial winds

Dance with the children's secret adventures

Surrounded by joyous untold stories

Hints of steaming goods and plenty more

Blazes of the campfire whip memorable glories.

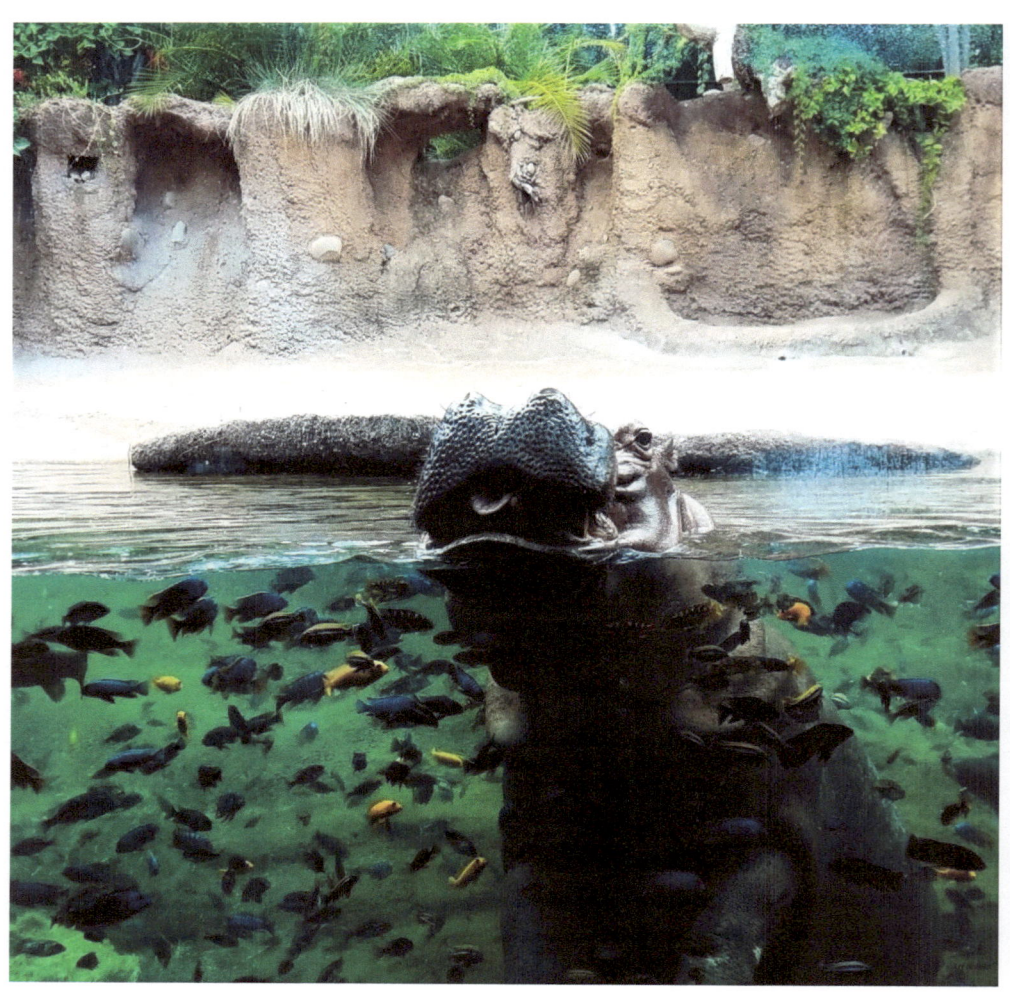

Children of Valencia City

Most have grown up that never left their own children's table.

Roaming the old ruins of historical value.

The need to belong to the same groups with personal labels.

Please remember, cause growth of the first edible diverse seed for your future.

The love I have for the children inspires more prayers.

Youth dreams of bright, brilliant, and self-sustaining agricultural sources.

Many drive to flourish with their unique attributes and desires.

Hope deriving from children who find challenges along the way to the intended connection.

Even though the same messages appear on the roaming walls with earthen paints.

When hate or anger arises, the emotions become wasted for a chaos' chance.

Girls and boys sometimes learn truth is better than a lie, a tiny bit late.

Where roses bloom with baby's breath and crows fly from the net that is cast.

The old child games collide with the new child games and diversity flourishes.

Where we saw the corporate tower, children saw the decayed loft from a great-grandmother

When our adventure begins, a child's outlook always begins with the spiritual journey within

After all, their hearts only know what's safe and familiar from Mother Nature.

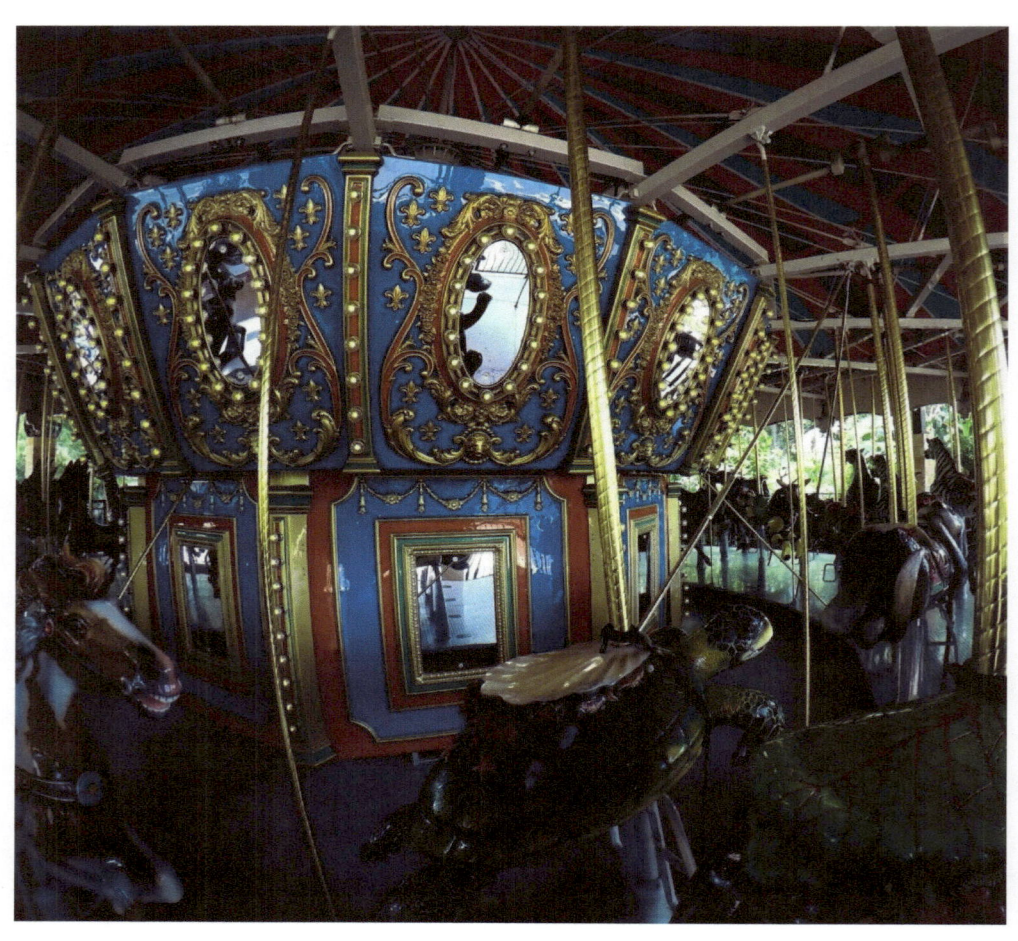

Ninth Worldly View

It's just different, that's all.

Rules are a guidance for our brothers' and sisters' adulthood.

Protected by the deadliest, gaseous, cosmic fireballs.

Living with the breath the beauty of the floral excretes amidst holy petrified wood.

Such a forgiving universe full of custom pathways and black holes.

My heart rejuvenates and strengthens in the liquid of silence.

The essence existing inside maneuvers through all challenges that unfold.

For whom doesn't understand, will not dare to attempt steps on fragile lens.

Moments of blissful solitude blend with gathering of friends.

Deep sleep finds energy to sustain subconscious enchantment

Visual images bring forth stories of curiosity for the mind to trance in.

Overseeing daily growth in personal achievement.

View so sweet to taste.

In eternity, thoughts reside in the heart of it all to have unwavering service toward each other.

Steading the pace to handle the burdens of cries from the multitude of races.

Answers help resolve and lift the heavy weight to move forward.

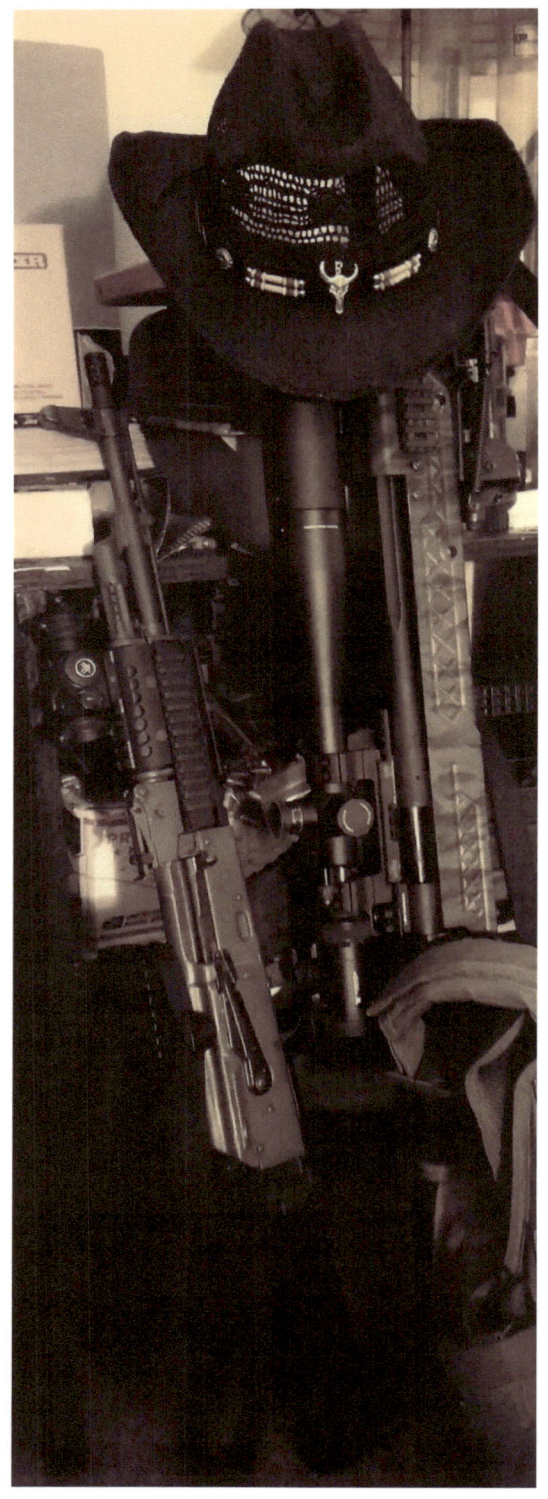

From Prayer to You

It is a gift in itself that replenishes your plate.
When the angel truly stays by your side.
Guarantees to have no lies, in any condition or life phase or state.
Keeps close to the holy spirit and keeps love in mind.

To rest your beloved soul from chaos.
Letting the demons dissipate to the black holes.
There is a value, a wonder, a special kaleidoscope of you that isn't lost.
As your love wakes me up each morning and a strength that bores.

Leave the worn book by the bedside table under adoring eyes.
The good word to provide comfort and shield from unnatural desires.
Listening to the beloved grandfather's tale at night.
Provides enriching dreams of marshmallow pillows swelling higher.

The kindness behind your loving touch on my heart.
Knowing others feel the love in me for you.
To share what follows beyond the grave, a blessed spirit lurks.
My thoughts, my words, and my emotions burst with truth.

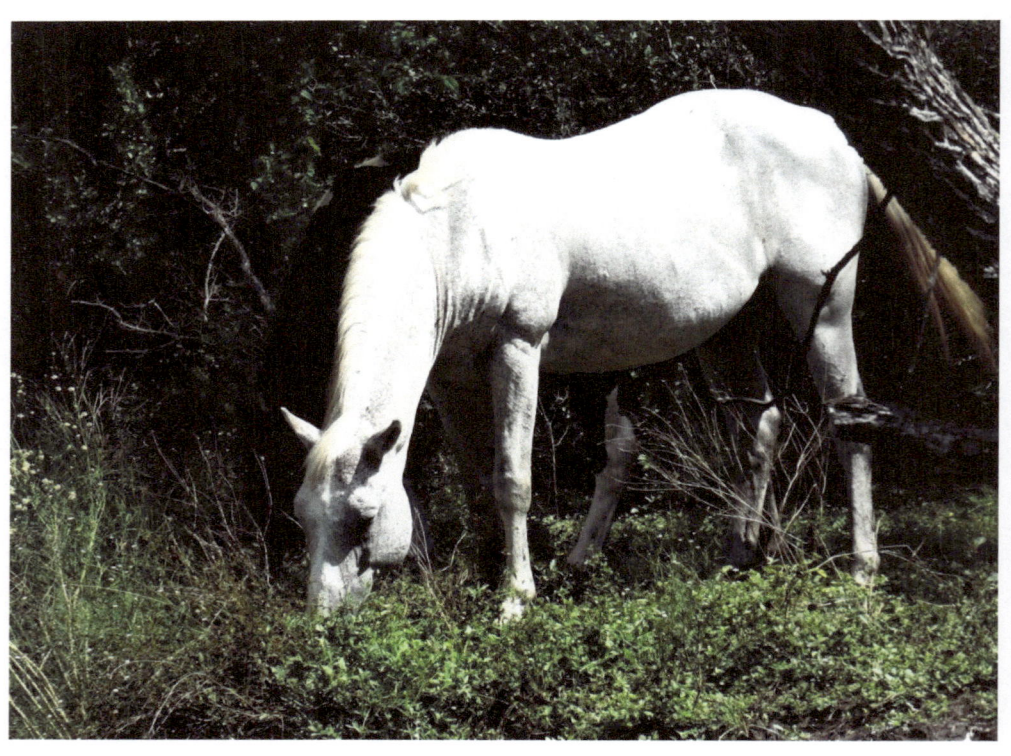

Love Echoing Us
By Annette V. Cantu

With music from the best orchestras

Dances connect the soul's emotion

He knows my love and she knows my love.

It's such a simple request and an inescapable, spiritual, devotion.

Thumping and pattering along the glorious dreams.

 Mesmerized by the spirit's touch of kindness.

Abundance of forgiving gestures and healing memories to keep.

Understanding the eternal wings and blessings.

Gentle nudges of happiness fills the beating chambers.

Singing in rejoice for the unique praises.

Lifted by my soul-mates' cares,

Eternity of support naturally resides in love's wake.

His loving memories and her loving memories stay with me forever.

Water reflects the glow we have and mimics cherished moments.

The flowers cascade in abundance with each time we are together.

Ringing in quiet celebrations and sharing streams of feelings on the wisps of feathers.

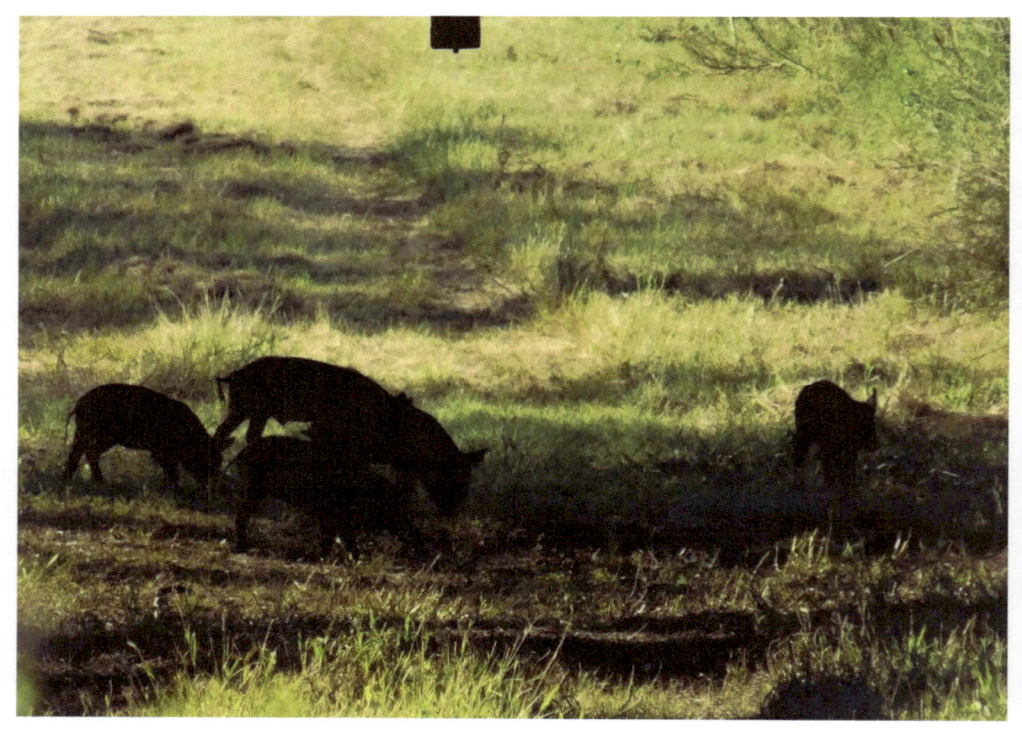

Didn't Expect their Kind (1995-1/01/17)

The white with the blue full of hate.

The black with the brown full of anger.

The illegal activities from foreign entities pouring in by the unstamped crates.

The people who always enjoy murderous verbal and physical assaults on souls of the newborns.

The people who want to lie by the devil.

The people who ignore the holy spiritual realm.

The people who use every ounce of cause and effect to wreak hell.

The people who love to see blood spill and want to cause a fall.

I was not familiar with this allowable process in life.

It's sad that these people can't enjoy the Almighty Lord whom provides if they just behave.

For the realm of the physical is different from the realm of the spiritual that bores no strife.

When we see, the spirits see more, and hiding from fear isn't an option for all of the brave.

I miss the old kindhearted, and the ones that give a damn that do not follow animal drives.

Against those who don't want to accomplish more for their brothers and sisters.

Those who have the hardest time moving in rhythm with blessings of the ultimate divine.

What primal instinct holds the loving soul down that causes painful tears?

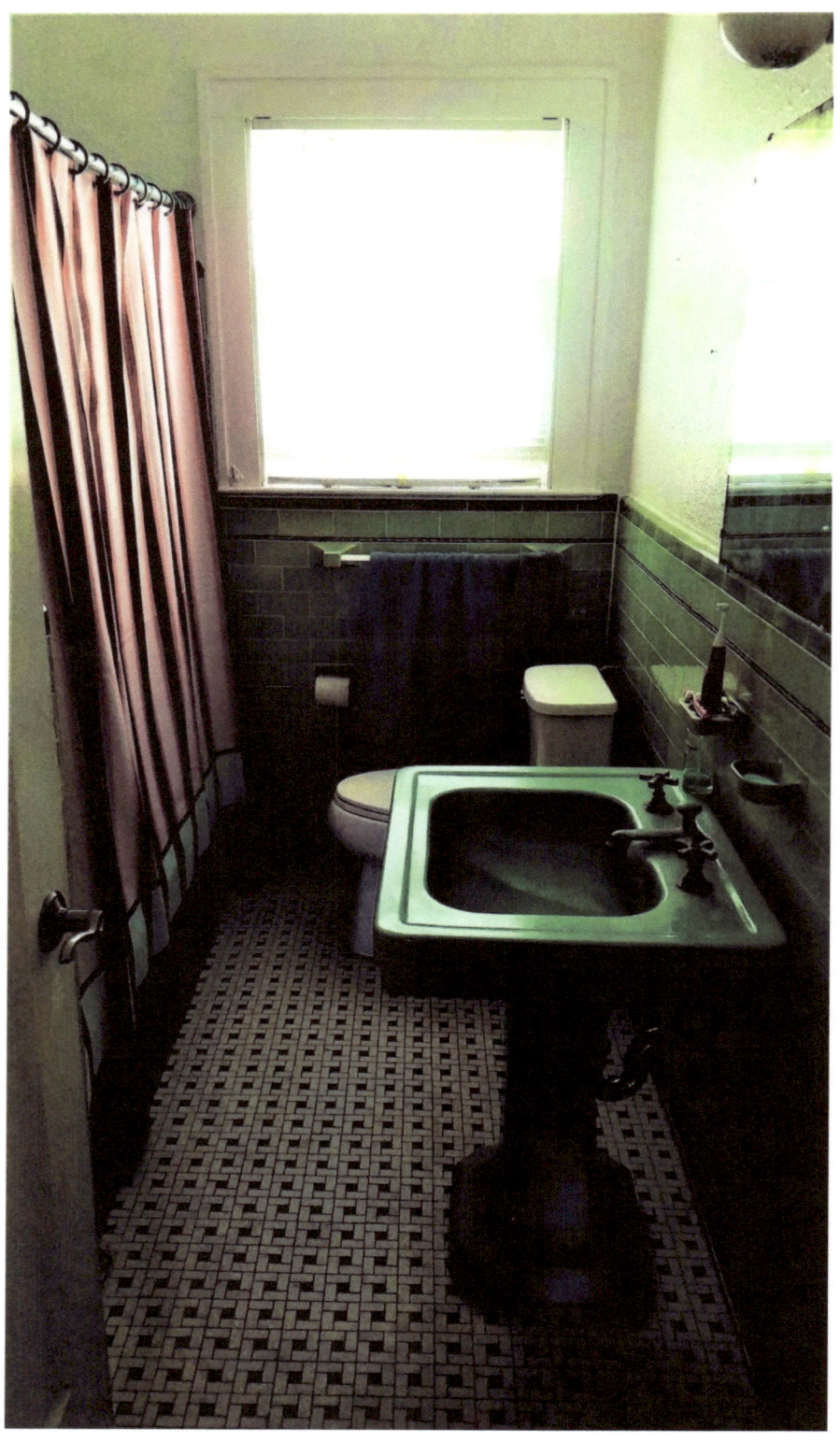

A Finer Life than Mine

Sky so blue and clear for me to take a deep breath to breathe

Landscapes unfold to reveal green pastures and welcoming homes

As my creative juices churned the worlds to bring forth beauty

Breathtaking colors vivid under a warm sun, feeling serenity, and love.

Night fills with stars to sing and felt safe on the swing.

Pain doesn't exist here and knowledge continues to flourish.

Conversations of intelligence takes place above the wings.

People show love here and true kindness on the whim.

Even the animals come to play with me, bringing joy.

From nostalgic grey hounds to the purrs of tiny tigers.

Ancestors, family members, resolve their messages with good girls and boys.

Every moment counts and is savored.

Sleeping on the safety of prayers.

Weight of countless gold bars lift me to secure my head with the gracious spirit.

Rejuvenated from the angels' song, playing the music with care.

Free marble rooms with a fireplace and warm cuisines with a healthy drink.

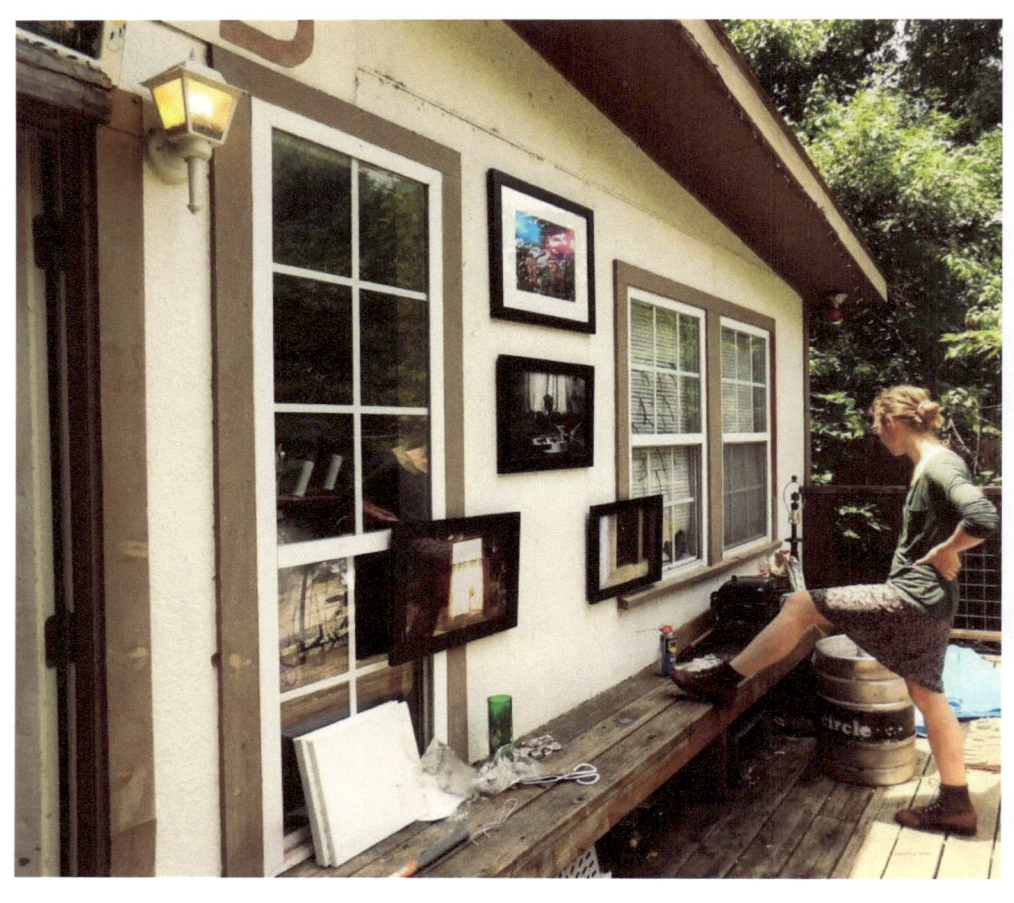

Searching Beyond My Skin

I thought the lightly burnish colored skin was once beautiful

Nowadays trying to appease the coldest ancient Lord beyond the wearable surface

The *Children of the Village of the Damned* taught me well from stories they told.

Now, mindful to search beyond the blood flowing through my veins.

Turns out I was not a slave, and yet the tan makes for an unwanted manipulative excuse.

My intellect rivals the ancient philosophies, and yet the darker tone undesirably thrives.

Even after the idolizing doesn't stop, scientists admire the diversity to use.

Understanding my genetics' development and living in nature's desire.

When the mentally induced psychos come out to play and take a look

All that I am capable of doing is welcome and pray my code is fine for each one.

Somehow each one sees my pain and concocts another scheme for the general cook.

Advising, how my choice of skin is fine when not hurt by the stun.

When blessings beam between those that love me.

Ecstatic shock creates the surprise needed to wake from another's dream.

After every day of searching the world, to replenish from sweet treats,

My beauty is honored by the loving eyes reflected with cherished greetings.

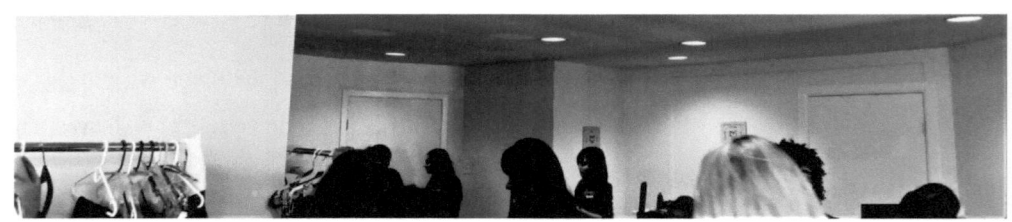

Central Law's Touch

Justice does its job when there is not a selfish corruptive act.

Along the fine lines printed by each American publisher.

As I am capable of browsing the aged documents for protection and to understand.

To eliminate the wild hatred, tame the idiocrasy, to not mislead him, and to assist her.

Enjoying the company of each man and woman who celebrate the laws for caring

Embellishing in happiness from each truthful answer laid out by the untainted courts.

Willing to take in all of the verbal, factual, and emotional evidence for clarity.

So that the souls may be at peace, rest, and not forlorn.

Every time, I read the laws of the land and understand all the wars that raged

My respect grows for those who help me survive and whom have allowed me to be conceived.

Who could deny a new soul the freedom of life's rewards, even when each of us ages?

Despite all the tears from the unwanted pain and another's negative beliefs.

And before I have the right to sleep

My soul is comforted to know upon wake, I am protected.

And after I have the right to a full night's sleep

Looking forward to another successful generation living life to the fullest.

www.ingramcontent.com/pod-product-compliance
Lightning Source LLC
Chambersburg PA
CBHW040235220526
45473CB00001B/249